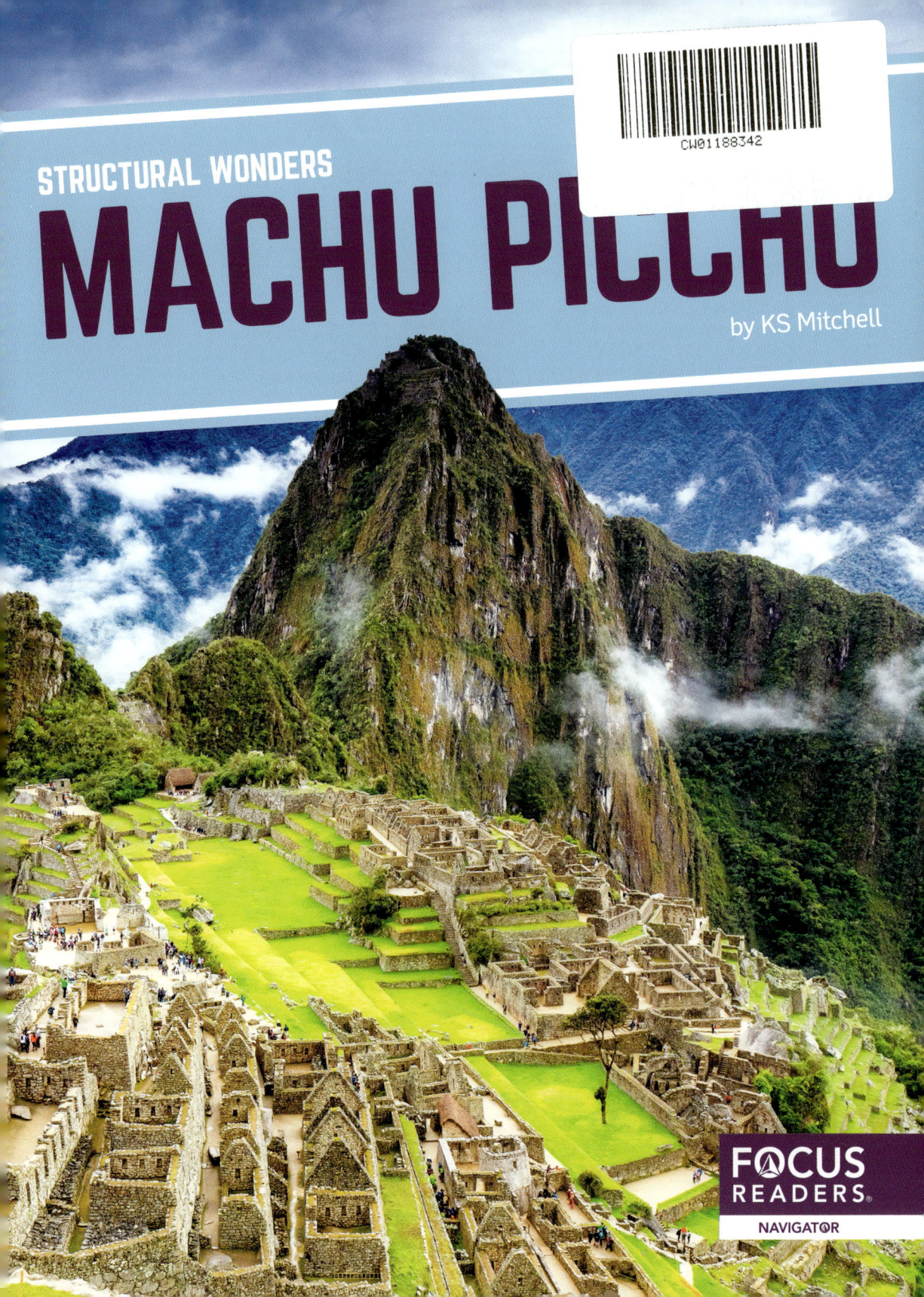

WWW.FOCUSREADERS.COM

Copyright © 2023 by Focus Readers®, Lake Elmo, MN 55042. All rights reserved. No part of this book may be reproduced or utilized in any form or by any means without written permission from the publisher.

Focus Readers is distributed by North Star Editions:
sales@northstareditions.com | 888-417-0195

Produced for Focus Readers by Red Line Editorial.

Photographs ©: Shutterstock Images, cover, 1, 4–5, 6, 9, 10–11, 13, 17, 23, 24–25, 26, 29; Rainer Lesniewski/Alamy, 15; Peter Langer/Danita Delimont Photography/Newscom, 18–19; Lordprice Collection/Alamy, 21

Library of Congress Cataloging-in-Publication Data
Names: Mitchell, KS, author.
Title: Machu Picchu / by KS Mitchell.
Description: Lake Elmo, MN : Focus Readers, 2023. | Series: Structural wonders | Includes index. | Audience: Grades 4-6
Identifiers: LCCN 2022034508 (print) | LCCN 2022034509 (ebook) | ISBN 9781637394816 (hardcover) | ISBN 9781637395189 (paperback) | ISBN 9781637395875 (pdf) | ISBN 9781637395554 (ebook)
Subjects: LCSH: Machu Picchu Site (Peru)--Juvenile literature.
Classification: LCC F3429.1.M3 M57 2023 (print) | LCC F3429.1.M3 (ebook) | DDC 985/.37--dc23/eng/20220720
LC record available at https://lccn.loc.gov/2022034508
LC ebook record available at https://lccn.loc.gov/2022034509

Printed in the United States of America
Mankato, MN
012023

ABOUT THE AUTHOR

Kimberly (KS) Mitchell is the author of the Pen & Quin: International Agents of Intrigue series and other books for kids and young adults. She writes, runs, and reads from Portugal.

TABLE OF CONTENTS

CHAPTER 1
City of Stone 5

CHAPTER 2
Building Machu Picchu 11

THAT'S AMAZING!
Temple of the Sun 16

CHAPTER 3
Inca Culture 19

CHAPTER 4
Visiting the Ruins 25

Focus on Machu Picchu • 30
Glossary • 31
To Learn More • 32
Index • 32

CHAPTER 1

CITY OF STONE

A hidden city stands atop a misty mountain. Stone buildings crisscross the steep slope. Some of the buildings have collapsed. Fog swirls around the ruins. Green **terraces** lead down the mountain's side. They look like giant stairs. The site is called Machu Picchu. It was built by the Incas more

Machu Picchu is often foggy in the early morning, but it tends to clear up by the afternoon.

A modern statue of Pachacuti, the Inca ruler, stands near Machu Picchu.

than 500 years ago. But it remains a structural wonder.

Machu Picchu is nestled high in the Andes Mountains. It lies 50 miles (80 km) northwest of Cusco, Peru. Cusco was the capital city of the Inca Empire. In the early 1500s, the Incas ruled a large part of South America.

Machu Picchu was not a typical Inca city. Most **archaeologists** think it was built for Pachacuti, an Inca emperor. The city features palaces and temples. So, it was probably an important religious site.

PACHACUTI

In the early 1400s, the Incas controlled only a small area around Cusco. At the time, Pachacuti's father, Viracocha, was the Inca leader. According to Inca stories, invaders attacked Cusco in 1438. Viracocha fled the city to stay safe. However, Pachacuti stayed in Cusco to fight. He led a group that defeated the invaders. After that, Pachacuti became the new Inca leader. He ruled for more than 30 years.

Machu Picchu sits between two mountain peaks. The ruins are about 7,710 feet (2,350 m) above sea level. A footpath connects the city to a river far below. This river winds its way through a valley.

For many years, archaeologists thought Machu Picchu was built around 1450. However, scientists studied skeletons found at the site. These bones dated back to 1420. So, people may have been living at Machu Picchu even earlier than archaeologists first thought.

In 1983, Machu Picchu became a World Heritage Site. That means the site has great value to people all around the world.

The Urubamba River flows for approximately 450 miles (725 km). It eventually becomes part of the Amazon River.

In 2007, Machu Picchu was voted one of the New Seven Wonders of the World. The ruins draw visitors from all over the globe. And scientists are still trying to learn more about this amazing structure.

CHAPTER 2

BUILDING MACHU PICCHU

Construction of Machu Picchu took place in the 1400s. Like many cities, Machu Picchu was built near water. First, the builders found a **spring** on a mountain slope. Next, they made a canal out of stone. This canal brought water toward the spot where the city would be built.

Canals carried clean water to several fountains within the city.

After that, workers started constructing the buildings. They had a **quarry** at the top of the mountain. That way, they didn't have to haul the massive stones very far. Workers cut each stone carefully and precisely. The pieces fit together perfectly. When stacked, they stayed

DANCING STONES

Earthquakes are common in Peru. They can destroy buildings. But Machu Picchu was designed to survive them. Its buildings were constructed without **mortar**. When an earthquake strikes, each stone can move slightly. The stones almost seem to dance. When the earthquake is over, the stones settle back into place. The building stays standing.

Machu Picchu's terraces allow rainwater to drain down the mountain without causing landslides or flooding.

together tightly. Each building also had a roof made of straw.

Machu Picchu is divided into two main sections. The agricultural section is made up of terraces. These flat areas look like a huge staircase carved into the mountain. Farmers grew crops on the terraces.

That way, people didn't have to haul as much food up the mountain.

The urban section is where most of the buildings are. The Main Plaza lies in the middle. On one side of the plaza, there are many simple homes. The people who served the emperor lived here. On the other side of the plaza, religious ceremonies took place. This area includes the most famous sites at Machu Picchu. For example, the Temple of the Sun is here. The Temple of the Three Windows is also on this side.

When people arrived at Machu Picchu, they entered through the Sun Gate. This gate was built to line up with the rising sun on the summer **solstice**. Inside the city is a large stone called the Intihuatana. This stone may have been used as a **sundial**. It could have helped people keep track of the seasons.

MAP OF MACHU PICCHU

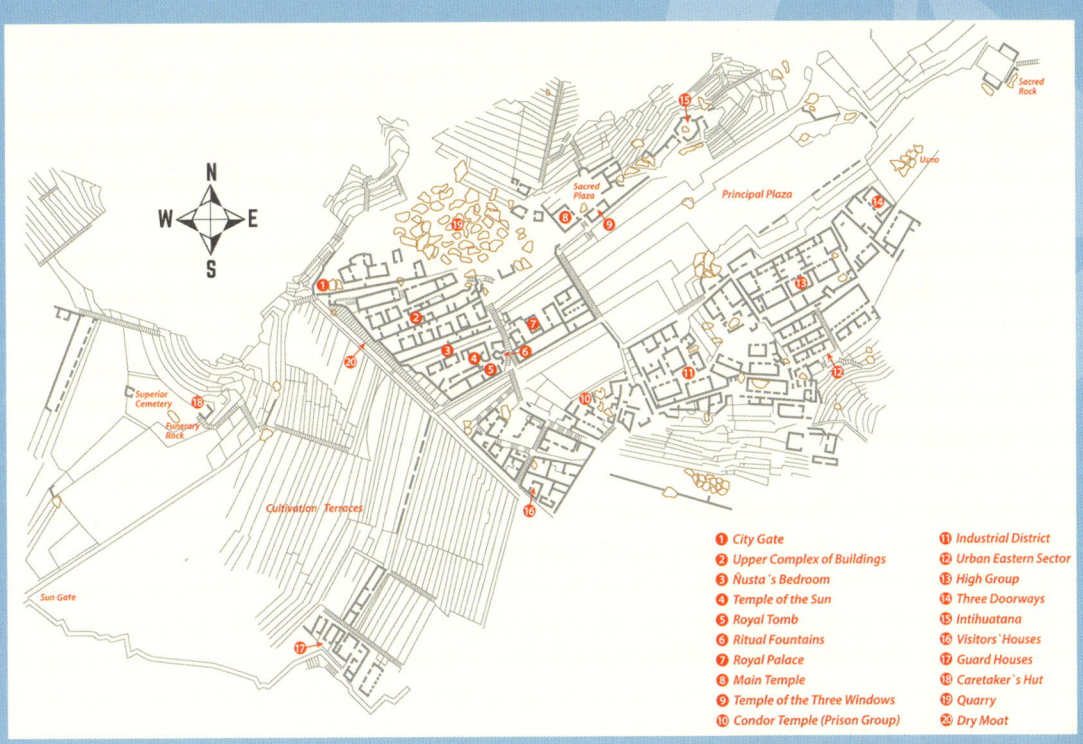

1. City Gate
2. Upper Complex of Buildings
3. Ñusta´s Bedroom
4. Temple of the Sun
5. Royal Tomb
6. Ritual Fountains
7. Royal Palace
8. Main Temple
9. Temple of the Three Windows
10. Condor Temple (Prison Group)
11. Industrial District
12. Urban Eastern Sector
13. High Group
14. Three Doorways
15. Intihuatana
16. Visitors´ Houses
17. Guard Houses
18. Caretaker`s Hut
19. Quarry
20. Dry Moat

THAT'S AMAZING!

TEMPLE OF THE SUN

Many Inca cities had temples for gods. In the Inca religion, Inti was the sun god. He was especially important to farmers. That's because the sun helps crops grow.

At Machu Picchu, the Temple of the Sun is one of the best-known structures. The temple is shaped like a semicircle. It has two windows. Scientists think the Incas used them to observe solstices. The first window lined up with the rising sun on the winter solstice. The second window lined up with the sun on the summer solstice.

The temple has an altar inside. Here, priests made sacrifices to worship Inti. They also used the temple as a sort of calendar. It was based on the sun's movement. And it guided many events.

Only priests and other high-ranking people were allowed inside the Temple of the Sun.

For example, it told people when to plant and harvest crops. It also determined when they held religious festivals.

CHAPTER 3

INCA CULTURE

The Incas did not have a writing system. For this reason, archaeologists aren't exactly sure when Inca society began. But the Incas probably formed their capital city of Cusco in the 1100s.

For many years, the Incas were a small group. They stayed near Cusco. That changed in the 1400s. The Incas started

The Incas used knotted strings called *quipu* to record information.

attacking and stealing from nearby groups. They also took these people's land. Over time, they started to form an empire.

Pachacuti became the Inca ruler in 1438. He expanded the empire even more. He also ordered many temples and fortresses to be built. One of them was Machu Picchu.

By 1530, the Inca Empire covered much of South America's western coast. The empire included 10 million people. Most of these people were not Incas. They were groups that the Incas had conquered. Inca leaders ruled over these people. They made them pay taxes.

The name Pachacuti means "World-Shaker" in the Quechua language.

They also forced people to follow the Incas' religion and **culture**. In addition, they made people speak Quechua, the Incas' language.

Spanish **colonists** attacked the Incas in 1532. The invaders spread many diseases. Up to 90 percent of the

Inca population may have died. As a result, the Inca Empire fell apart quickly. The Spanish took control.

The Incas had already abandoned Machu Picchu when the Spanish invaded. Archaeologists aren't sure why. Some think the city didn't have enough water.

INCA ROADS

The Incas built thousands of miles of roads. The most famous road is the Inca Trail. It leads to Machu Picchu. The Incas' roads allowed soldiers to move easily through the empire. There were many stations along the way. Messengers ran from one station to the next. They delivered important news. The Incas also built rope bridges. These bridges helped people cross narrow valleys with steep sides.

Farmers at Machu Picchu raised llamas for their fur and meat.

Others think the Incas left because of a disease. Whatever the case, the Spanish never found Machu Picchu. As the years passed, the city became overgrown. Local people continued to farm on the terraces. But the site remained unknown to outsiders.

CHAPTER 4

VISITING THE RUINS

For hundreds of years, few people knew that Machu Picchu existed. But in 1911, an American archaeologist visited Peru. Local guides showed him Machu Picchu. The archaeologist began studying the ruins. News of his work spread around the world. Machu Picchu soon became famous.

In total, there are approximately 170 buildings at Machu Picchu.

 Some parts of the Inca Trail are built along steep cliffs.

By the late 1900s, Machu Picchu was a major tourist attraction. Now, more than one million people visit every year. Most people arrive by train from Cusco. However, some people hike to Machu Picchu along the Inca Trail.

26

Tourism brings huge amounts of money to Peru. But it also creates problems. For example, not all visitors treat Machu Picchu with respect. Some people climb the walls. Others take stones from the site. And in 2000, the Intihuatana stone was damaged during the filming of a TV commercial.

Machu Picchu faces environmental dangers, too. Earthquakes, heavy rain, and mudslides are common in the area. These events can damage the site. They are also dangerous to tourists. In 2010, mudslides trapped thousands of people near Machu Picchu. They were rescued by helicopter.

For years, archaeologists said the huge number of visitors was a problem. They asked Peru's government to reduce the number of people at the site. In 2022, the government put limits on how many people were allowed to visit Machu Picchu each day. Also, visitors could not

WRONG NAME?

Machu Picchu gets its name from one of the mountain peaks near the site. In the Quechua language, *Machu Picchu* means "Old Mountain." In the 1910s, this name became world famous. But in 2021, a researcher discovered it is probably the wrong name. The Incas most likely called the site Huayna Picchu. That's the name of the other peak near the ruins. It means "New Mountain."

Part of the Main Temple became damaged due to the soil and weather.

enter without a guide. Archaeologists hoped these changes would help. They wanted people to enjoy Machu Picchu for many years to come.

FOCUS ON
MACHU PICCHU

Write your answers on a separate piece of paper.

1. Write a letter to a friend describing the main ideas of Chapter 2.

2. Do you think Peru's government should limit the number of people at Machu Picchu? Why or why not?

3. When did Spanish colonists invade the Inca Empire?
- **A.** 1438
- **B.** 1532
- **C.** 1911

4. What is the most likely reason that many of Machu Picchu's buildings are still standing?
- **A.** The Incas hired many workers to repair them.
- **B.** The area does not get many earthquakes.
- **C.** The buildings were constructed without mortar.

Answer key on page 32.

GLOSSARY

archaeologists
People who study the ancient past, often by digging up buildings or objects from long ago.

colonists
People who settle in a new place and take control.

culture
The way a group of people live; their customs, beliefs, and laws.

mortar
A material that holds bricks or stones together.

quarry
A pit where stone is dug up from the ground.

solstice
The time when one of Earth's hemispheres has its longest or shortest day of the year.

spring
A place where water comes out of the ground.

sundial
A device that tells time based on the shadow it creates.

terraces
Flat areas of land cut into hills or mountains so farmers can grow crops.

TO LEARN MORE

BOOKS

Alkire, Jessie. *Exploring Ancient Cities.* Minneapolis: Abdo Publishing, 2019.

Golkar, Golriz. *Science of Machu Picchu.* North Mankato, MN: Capstone Press, 2023.

Weitzman, Elizabeth. *Mysteries of Machu Picchu.* Minneapolis: Lerner Publishing, 2018.

NOTE TO EDUCATORS

Visit **www.focusreaders.com** to find lesson plans, activities, links, and other resources related to this title.

INDEX

agricultural section, 13
Andes Mountains, 5–6, 8, 11–14, 28

canal, 11
Cusco, Peru, 6–7, 19, 26

erosion, 27

Inca people, 5–7, 16, 19–23, 28

Inca Trail, 22, 26
Intihuatana, 15, 27

Pachacuti, 7, 20
preservation, 28–29

Quechua, 21, 28

religious ceremonies, 7, 14, 16–17
river, 8

South America, 7, 20
Spanish colonists, 21–23
stones, 5, 11–12, 15, 27

Temple of the Sun, 14, 16–17
terraces, 5, 13, 23
tourism, 26–29

urban section, 14

Answer Key: 1. Answers will vary; 2. Answers will vary; 3. B; 4. C